# Generis

PUBLISHING

# *FOLLOW ME*

*Arthur Cimwanga Badibanga*

**CIP a Camerei Naționale a Cărții**

**Cimwanga, Badibanga Arthur.**

Follow me / Arthur Cimwanga Badibanga – Chişinău : Generis Publishing, 2020 (Print on demand). – 57 p.

Referințe bibliogr.: p. 56.

ISBN 978-9975-154-55-0.

811.111'36 C 49

Cover image: www.pexels.com/ru-ru/photo/4861377/
Audio Book:
https://drive.google.com/file/d/1Zbv3r0Zd0bRr7ANY50nHhAuzwdwc_hmp/view?usp=drive_web

Generis Publishing
Online orders: www.generis-publishing.com
Orders by email: info@generis-publishing.com

# Sommaire

# Dedication

To the youth all over the world

# Acknowledgements

I acknowledge Vlir-Unikis Academic English Laboratory club-mates for their warmful contribution to the production of this booklet.

Arlene Botchaka, Bijoux Gumete, Albert Bwato, Douce Olinda, Vanessa Lisako, and Jane Tshiyoyo deserve particular thanks for bringing out their voices and expertise for the achievement of this text.

Pol Cuvelier, Ank Lou and Tom Smith have brought their contribution with various materials worth using for a better text writing. They are kindly invited to the feast.

You too, are welcome, for unconscious data lent to the author.

**Arthur Cimwanga Badibanga Shambuyi**

# Welcome to English programme

## Follow me/ First edition

## Chapter One: Greetings

## 1.a. Formal greetings (Official or formal)

1.Good morning Sir – Good morning lady

2.Good evening Sarah- Ah good evening

3. -Good afternoon Liz – Good afternoon Dicta

4.How are you I am fine thank you

5.Good night - Good night my friend

6.How are you my dear: Just fine, thank you and you

 Fine too

7.How are you Jane? - Fine thanks and you Sam

8.How are you Algor? -I'm fine thank you Smith

9.How are you Matthew ? -Just great Anna

10.How are you Maguy ? Not bad my dear

**Melody**

**Practice: You meet different authorities, propose formal greetings to each of them.**

## 1.b.Informal greetings ( to use among friends, mates and colleagues)

1. Nice to meet you Johny-

 Nice to meet you Clarence

2. How is it going Mary ? Very well indeed

3.Tell me what 's up Kingstone?

 Just great dear Destino

4.How's it going with you Liz ?

 Nothing special

3. Tell me, how is Douce ?

 She is dealing quiet well

4. What's news Rogers ?

Great Brenda

5. By now, what's wrong with you Christelle?

 Not much Christevie

6. How' is the family Schola ?

 Good Benie

7. What's the matter Bea ?

 I am feeling bad two days ago Noella

8. Ehi Clemence how do you do –

 Ah yeah Alberte how do you do

9.Nice to meet you Madam!

 Nice to meet you Sir

10.Meeting you is a joy Francis!

 Oh It is a big joy to see you Jos

11.Hello my friend how do you do

 Hello how do you do

12.Hi my guy

 Hi my mate

13.How is the family?

Everybody keeps better

 14.How is it going with you?

 I am very well, thank you

15.Hoo and how are children

They are dealing well thank you

Song/Melody

**Practice: Refer to informal greetings and welcome your guests especially mates, colleagues, friends, or relatives ( members of the family)**

## 1.c. What is a greeting?

Sandra: A greeting is wish of good things Arlen

Arlen: Hum of good things you say Sandra?

Sandra: Yeah a greeting is a prayer, it is a kind of prayer, to always wish good things to someone

Arlen: Can you give one, two or three examples of greetings, or wishes/ w i s h i:z/

Sandra: Yes I can Arlen

Arlen: Come on Sandra

Sandra: Example: Good morning, good application, Good appetite, good job, good trip

Arlen: Okay you're right, thank you Sandra

Sandra: You're welcome Arlen

**Song /Melody**

## 1.d. Spelling / English alphabet

Bijoux: Eh Douce, how many phonemes counts English alphabet ?

Douce : English alphabet counts twenty six phonemes

Bijoux: Can you count them Douce ?

Douce : Yes , I can

Bijoux: Just do it Douce

Douce : Ok they are :

a b c d e f g h i j k l m n o p q r s t u v w x y z or American / z i:/

Bijoux: Ah yes

A / e i / as in pay

B / b i : / as in beat

C/ s i : / as in city

D/ d i : / as in dig

E/ i : / as in eat

F/ e f / as in foot

G / g i : / as in rigid

H /e i th/ as in hat

I / ai/ as in line / l a i n/

J / g e i/ as in journey

K /k e i /as in kettle

L/ e l/ as in leg

M /e m/ as in men

N /e n/as in neck

O /o/as in operation

P / p i: / as in people

Q / kyu:/ as in quick

R / a : / as in road

S / e s /as in school

T / t i : /as in tea

U / y u : /as in university

V/ v i : / as in village

W / d a b l y u :/as in water

X / e k s / as in text

Y / w a i / as in yesterday

Z/ z e d/ American / z i : / as in zoo / z o u : /

Douce: Congratulations

Bijoux: Welcome Douce

Douce: Good bye

Bijoux : Bye bye

**Song /Melody**

# Chapter Two: Willing to know your name

1.What is your name please ? – My name is Cimwanga Adaletale , and you ? My name is Cimwanga Milembo

2.Who are you ? I am Cimwanga Adaletale and you who are you ? I am Cimwanga Milembo

3.What is your first name ? My first name is Cimwanga

4.What is your last name ? My last name is Adaletale

5.Cimwanga Adaletale, what is your prename ? My prename is Elizabeth and you what is your prename ? My prename is Gaston.

6. Is Kingstone your name ? No, Kingstone is my nickname – aah

7. And Liz is your nickname too ? Yes Liz is my nickname

**Melody**

**Review: what is your name means who are you.**

**Practice: In your terms, try to know your classmate or your trip-mate**

# Chapter Three: What are you ? /Who are you

## 3.a. What are you ? It means what is, your job, your activity, your function

1.Ah Benie what are you ? I am a pupil and you Sam what are you ? I am a student

2.What is your father ? My father is a businessman and yours? My father is farmer

3.What is your mother ? She is a nurse and yours? My mother is a teacher

4.Ohhh

**Song /Melody**

**Review : What are you ? What is your job? What is your activity ? What is your function ?**


## 3.b Who are you ?


1. Who are you ? I am Senga and you who are you ? I am Dunga

2.Who is she ? She is Cilongo and that one, who is she? She is Sifa

3.Who is that guy over there? That is Nonda, He is Nonda

4.Who am I and what amI ? You are Cimwanga, you are a Professor

5.Who are you and what are you ? I am Menga, I am a businessman

6.Who is she and what is she ?Oh she is Nzinga , she is a businesswoman

7. Who is he and what is he ? Ah he is Kambale, he is a student

**3.C Where are you now ?**

-I am at University and you ? //Oh I am at University too.

-Where do you dwell ? //I dwell on Mulamba avenue number five and you

- I live on Campus, Shaumba dormitory the first floor number ten.

-And your girl-friend, where does she live ?//Sorry, it is private, excuse me

-Eh, my dear too jealous //Of course, you too//Frankly we are the same.

- How do you do //How do you do

# Chapter Four: Asking direction

1.  Where do you come from ? I come from home, and you ? I come from the market

2.  And your sister, where does she come from ? She comes from University

3.  Where does your father come from ? He comes from Nairobi

4.  Where do your mother and your sister come from ? They come from church

5.  Eh Chistelle, where from ? From Campus and you Christevie, where from ? From hospital

a.  Then where do you go Jos ? I go to the University and you Mary. I go to the beach

b.  King, where does your brother go ? He goes to England

c.  Tell me Destino, where do your parents go ? They go to South-Africa

d.  Eh Becker, where to ? To school, and you Benie where to ? To the cinema

**Practice: Propose a short text asking directions**

**Melody**

# Chapter Five : Means of transport

1. Jane, how do you go to University ? I go to University by car

2.And you Prisca, how do you to University ? I go University by bicycle

3.How do Boyoma people travel to Kinshasa ?

Some people travel by plane or by boat

4.Do Boyoma inhabitants go to Ubundu by boat too? No, they go to Ubundu by train, by lorries, by motor-cycle or simply by bicycle.

5.How do you often go to church . We often go to church on foot.

**Melody**

6.Is there any train for Central Kongo ?Yes there is

7.Can I catch the train Ilebo Lubumbashi via Kananga ? Indeed you can

8.I used to travel by train from Bumba to Isiro via Aketi and Buta , but now, sorry!!!

9.Oh yes Kinshasa internal train still works

10 There is no train from Kinshasa to Bandundu, but there is a boat from Mai-Ndombe to Ilebo

11.Mosolo travels to Basoko by canoe.

12.Canoeing is a perilous task

**Practice: Analyse different means of transport people refer to in DRC.**

# Chapter Six: My family

## 6.1 Biological family composition

1. What are members of your biological family? Members of my biological family are my father, my mother, my brothers and my sisters.

2. How many parents has your family ? My family has two parents, the father and the mother

3.How many sisters do you have ? I have seven sisters

4. How many brothers do you have? I have two brothers

5. What is the name of your father ? My father's name is Mensa Brenda

5.And the name of your mother ?My mother's name is Andale Lansa ,

**Melody**

how do you do

6. Ah ah nice how do you do

7. How do you do

**6.2.Some sorts of families**

-Can you cite another family apart from the biological family ?//Yes I can

 -Oh come on//I can mention a scientific family

-Will you enumerate some members of the scientific family//Of course

-Mention them if you can//Teachers, pupils or students,//You mean applicants ?

-That's right//Is it all ?//No, I add a professional family//Do you remember my family ? //Uh, I can guess// Which one ?//Smokers family//Not at all

- Bye sir // Bye

**Practice: Develop families (s) you belong to.**

# Chapter Seven: How old are you ?

- ✓ How old are you Chiquitita ? I am twenty four years old
- ✓ How old is your father ? My father is ninety seven
- ✓ And how old is your mother ? My mother is eighty
- ✓ How old is your elder brother ? My elder brother is thirty eight
- ✓ Tell me, how old are your twins ? They are one year old
- ✓ How old is cat ? It is three years old
- ✓ How is Menar ? He is young
- ✓ How is Fanita ? She is middle aged

**(Practice: In your family discuss of ages of relatives)**

# Chapter Eight: Days of the week

- ✓ How many days are there in a week ? There are seven days in a week
- ✓ Can you count seven days of a week ? yes I can,/ come on please: there are Monday, Tuesday, Wednesday, Thursday, Friday , Saturday , Sunday( he repeats)
- ✓ Where do people often go on Sunday ? On Sunday, people often go to church
- ✓ Oh yes, what is the first day of the week ? The first day of the week is Monday
- ✓ What is the second day of the week ? The second day of the week is Tuesday

6. What is the sixth day of the week ? The sixth day of the week is Saturday

**Melody**

**(Practice: Speak of daily common activities and use days and weeks)**

# Chapter Nine: Months of the year

How many months has a year ?// A year has twelve months

Can you count months of the year ?/Yes I can. Come on please : January, February, March, April, May, June, July, August, September, October, November, and December.( he repeats)

What is the second month of the week ? //The second month of the week is February

What is the fifth month of the year ? //The fifth month of the year is May.

And let me see, in which month is Christmas ? //Christmas is in December

In which month is new year ? //New year is in January

In which month is independence of DRC ?// Independence of DRC is in June

And lastly, I would like to ask you one question, in which month is your birthday ?//My birthday is in July

Oh good

**Melody**

**Practice: Think of some historical dates and initiate questions**

# Chapter Ten: Where do you live ?

Sam ,where do you live ?// I live in DRC//Where do you live in DRC ?

 I live in Tshopo Province//Where do you live in Tshopo Province ? /I live in Kisangani city

Where do you live in Kisangani city ? In Kisangani city I live on Kiwele boulevard n°2

In which quarter is Kiwele boulevard ?/ Oh Kiwele boulevard is in Boyoma plateau Makiso township

**Song**

**(Practice: Create a dialogue and use target expressions)**

# Chapter Eleven: Do you like it ?

Liz, do you like fish ? Yes I do, I like much fish

Oh good, do you like fresh meat Jane ? No I don't, because meats destroys my teeth/ huu do you want to mean that meat destroys your teeth…

Do you like potatoes ? Yes I do

Oh good, does your elder brother like pizza ? Yes he does Professor

Does your younger sister like porridge ? Of course she does

Do your parents like cassava bread and rice ? Of course they do

Do they like traveling by air ? Yes they do, they enjoy it

**Song /Melody**

**Practice: Ask similar questions and answer**

# Chapter Twelve : Wishes

A greeting is a wish and a wish is a prayer too

1.Today is my birthday ,

 2.Happy birthday Anna !

 3.Aah, you say, you mean today is also your birthday

 4.Yees

 5.Then I wish a happy birthday

 6.Thank you

 7..Ah good,

 8.Eh Mary enjoy your meal,
 9.likewise come with me Misenga
 10.Where do you go Mulamba ?
 11.To Europe!
 12.Uh Safe journey ;
 13.I'll need it
 14.Let me see, Samba I have examen soon at the faculty !
 15.waou, good luck my dear,
 16.Thanks
 17.We have English course by now ;
 18.Ok good application
 19. Thank you
**Melody**

**Practice: Express wishes in your terms to various people of your community**

# Chapter Thirteen: Adjectives and Adverbs

## a.  Adjectives

They are words that identify, quantify, describe, qualify or modify other words Adjectives are usually positioned before the <u>noun</u> or <u>pronoun</u> that they modify.

**ex:**

1.My **nice** teacher. **Nice** is adjective, teacher is a noun. Shada is my nice teacher. Ah good

2.Her **good** student. **Good** is adjective, Student is a noun. Mulenga is a good student

3.This **big** book. **Big** is adjective, and book is a noun. These are big books Okay.

**(b. Adverbs/**

*Just like adjectives , adverbs are modifiers or qualifiers*
 Examples)

4.My father drives, **slowly**, his car but my elder rides **quickly** his motor-bike

5.We **often** go to church on Sunday, but **sometimes** students study on the day off

6.She **scarcely** drinks whisky in parties

7. I, **personally**, don't like alcohol, my favourite drink is lemon**1.**

Let me tell you a remark: adjectives never change in English ,it is invariable for singular and plural, so do adverbs.

**Melody**

By now…chapter fourteen

## Chapter Fourteen : Size : How does he look ?

1.How does he look ? He is tall

2. And how does she look ? She is slim and beautiful

3.How do I look ? You are short and good-looking

4. How do look these twins ? They are medium height

5.How does look their mother ? Their mother is heavy because fat

6.And how does look her father ? He is thin and tall

7.How does look that girl ? She is weak and light

8.How does look that boy ? He is handsome and strong

9.How do look your sisters ? They are pretty and dark

10.How does look Sana ? Oh she is ugly

11. Waou

**Melody**

# Chapter Fifteen: Colours

a.How many principal colours do you know ?

b.I know seven principal colours and some secondary ones

a.Cite some main colours

b.Oh you need to know some main colours ?

a.Yes Sir

b. Oh I know blue, black, white, yellow, red, grey and green

a.Waou, congratulations

b. Thank you

**Melody**

# Chapter Sixteen: Conjunctions but, and, or …

1.Conjunctions of coordination: but, and, or. etc. (…) link objects and individuals of the same nature and the same function. They link two independent clauses.

 ex: Goats and pigs are animals.

 ex: Kingstone is a boy but Benedicte is a girl.

2. Conjunctions of subordination: as soon as, if, unless…

Ok, they link principal clauses to subordinate ones

ex: As soon as the professor enters the room, the course starts

Exercise: Now in terms of practice, make as many sentences as you can be using conjunctions studied here up.

 a. He is intelligent but talkative
 b. She is clever but ugly
 c. They are handsome and polite
 d. These girls are beautiful and pretty
 e. You get in or you stay out
 f. You can eat fish or meat
 g. Oh no, I like vegetables, rice and beans
 h. He drinks water because he is thirsty
 i. Shamy plays football but Elena plays basketball
 j.Oh yes How do you do
 k.How do you do

 **Melody**

# Chapter Seventeen: What do they do / where do they work?

**Nouns Verbs Activities**

A teacher to teach he teaches

An artist to draw he draws

A singer to sing he sings

A writer to write he writes

An engineer to design he designs technical projects

A manager to manage he manages office

A director to direct he directs

A cameraman to make films he makes tv programs or video

A businesswoman to do business she does business

A police officer to protect people he protects people

A sales assistant to sell things he sells things

A veterinarian to take care of animals he takes care of animals

A doctor to take care of people he takes care of people

An actor to act he acts

A waitress to serve food she serves food

A waiter to serve food he serves food

A computer programmer to program computer he programmes

An accountant to manage money he manages money

A student to study he studies

A football player to play football he plays football

**melody /Song**

## 6.4 Where do they work and Prepositions of place _at_ and _in ( repeat)_

*A. His Excellency Felix Antoine Tshisekedi Tshilombo*

*1. Where does he work ?*

2.*What does he do ?*

*B. His Excellency Marcel Utembi Tapa*

*1. Where does he work ?*

2.*What does he do ?*

*C. His Eminence Fridolin Ambongo*

1.*What does he do ?*
*D. Angela Merkel*
*1. Where does she work ?*
2.*What does he do ?*
*E. His Holy the Pope Francis*
*1. Where does he work ?*
2.*What does he do ?*
*F. The Queen Elizabeth II*
1.*Where does she work ?*
 2.*What does she do ?*
*G. His Excellency Donald Trump*
1.*Where does he work ? What does he do ?*

**Practice : Make up similar questions and propose answers with prepositions at and in.**

 **Melody/ Lucky Dube**

# Chapter Eighteen : Short phrases without conjugated verbs

A phrase is made of a group of words organized, which reveal a meaningful statement but does not necessarily contain a conjugated verb in it.

e.g In the name of the Father and of the Son and of the Holy Spirit .Amen.

e.g Where from my dear?

-From home and you.?

-From church

-Where to my friend '?

-To Edith-stein university college

-What for brother ?

-For a written quiz

-Which one ?

-For an English quiz

-Ok. Good luck, bye

-Bye bye.

**Practice: Compose your own meaningful text with simple phrases and make these exercises.**

**Song/Melody**

# Chapter Nineteen: Derivations

This linguistic system of derivations consists in adding some affixes to existing morphemes to form new words that may or may not be the same part of speech. Affixes can be added to a verb to have another verb, or to have a noun, to have an adjective or vice-versa.

ex:

Nation : noun / or substantive

Nations : substantive/ noun plural

National : adjective

Nationalism : noun

Nationality : noun

Nationalities : noun plural

Nationalist : noun

Nationalists : noun

Nationalisation : noun

Nationalisations : noun

International : adjective

Bi-national : adj of two nationalities

Ah you mean Bi-national is an adjective which refers to two nationalities ?

Yes ofcourse

Multinational: adjective: of many nationalities

Yes ofcourse

Ah good

Internationalisation: noun

Internationalisations : noun

We are going to continue next

**Song/Melody**

Nationalize : verb

Internationalize :verb

Internationalizers

Nationally : adv

*I hope we will continue next // Thanks a lot*

Thank you to

**Song/Melody**

*Practice: choose a concept and develop derivational affixes*

# **Chapter Twenty: Importance of English**

Tell me Douce, is English important for you?

Yes it is

Humm, explain me

 English is a world means of communication to link people

Ah ah, English is the first international language you say

 Yes , English is the first language of touring

Ok, English is the first scientific and literary language

Yes, English is the first language of sports

Is it all ?

No'

Come on Douce

English is the first language of diplomacy

English is the first language of computer and internet

Yes, English is also the language of music and culture/ k a l tcher/

They say, English is the first commercial language for business people

Ah ah congratulations then

Thank you

 **Song/ Melody**

**Practice: What is the importance of English in your life?**

# Chapter Twenty-One: DRC my country

*Nzita, what is the name of your country?*

*My country's name is Democratic Republic of Congo*

*Eh Cibangu, how many provinces counts your country ?*

*DRC counts twenty six provinces*

*Tell me, Chirimwina, is Maniema your province ?*

*No, Banza, my province is South Kivu and yours ? Is it Sankuru or Mongala ?*

*Neither Sankuru, nor Mongala,*

*What is it? Tell us*

*I am from Kabongo, my province is Upper Lomami*

*And you Bongilo, which province is yours?*

*I am from Yamofaya, my province is Tshopo*

*And ,how many territories counts Tshopo province ?*

*I think Tshopo province has seven territories*

*Can you enumerate them*

*Of course I can*

*Come on please Bongilo*

*Yes there are Bafwasende ,Banalia, Basoko, Isangi, Opala, Ubundu, and Yahuma*

*Is Kisangani a territory of Tshopo province ?*

*No, Kasereka, Kisangani is the country-town of Tshopo province*

*Are you able to cite two other country towns in DRC ?*

*Yes I am, the case of Lubumbashi in Upper Katanga, Matadi in Central Kongo*

 *Song/ Melody*

*a.Administrative Provinces of D R C*

*a.How many provinces counts DRC ?*

*b.They are twenty six*

*a.Waou, so many!*

*b.Not at all*

*a.Will you please cite administrative provinces of DRC ?*

*b.Of course, South Kivu, North Kivu, Maniema, Ituri, Upper Uélé, a.Lower Uélé, Tshopo, Mongala, Tshuapa, South Ubangi, North b.Ubangi, Equator, Tanganika, Upper Katanga, Lualaba, Upper Lomami, Lomami, Eastern Kasai, Western Kasai, Sankuru, Kasai,Central Kongo, Kuilu, Kwango, Mai-Ndombe and Kinshasa.*

*a.And you, what is your current province ?*

*b.Tshopo is .And you where do you dwell ?*

*a.Oh I am not anyone, I live in the capital , Kinshasa*

*b.Euh you must be lucky*

*a.You too, I still remember the mythical city of Kisangani with its Wagenia falls*

*b.Sure, each province has memorable and historical sites*

*a.Sincerely I like DRC*

*b.Naturally you should.*

# Chapter Twenty Two: Abstract concepts

*Abstracts words are different from concrete nouns because it cannot be seen nor touched*

*a.Can you recall some abstract concepts?*

*b.Yes I can*

*a.Just do it in a short phrase or sentence*

*b.Uhh, ok, Love is blind, love is abstract ( he repeats)*

*a.Ah you would like to say, love is blind, love is abstract*

*b.Yes of course*

*a.Continue*

*a..Life is a struggle, life is abstract*

*b..Another example*

*a..Kungu is very intelligent, intelligence is abstract*

*b. Ahh . It's enough congratulations*

 **Song//Melody**

# Chapter Twenty Three: Languages of DRC

*DRC is a large country with more than 450 tribal languages*

*There are four national languages Ciluba, Kikongo, Lingala, and Kiswahili*

*French and English play the role of official languages in DRC*

*The role of language is to link people and facilitate communication and so on. A ah yes…*

*Are still tribal languages important nowadays?*

*Yes, tribal languages are there to protect ancestral patrimony and cultural identities/ As an advice, do not lose your tribal language.*

*Is there any danger to forget one's tribal languages?*

*Of course, of course, If someone loses his mother tongue, he is uprooted.*

*Oh, what a pity*

*Hu huh u…*

***Song /Melody***

# Chapter Twenty-Four one: Human body's Parts

*Each part of the body plays a specific role.*

*Sorts of human body's devices: Internal and external parts*

**a.   External parts**

*Head, nose, eyes, ears, mouth, hair, hairs, fore head, hands, fingers, toes, nails, neck, chin, beards, chest, breasts, arm, bely, back, buttocks, thigh, leg, knee, ankle, foot, etc.*

*ex:*

*1. He shakes my hand*

*2.Mandanga covers her head with a scarf*

*3.We just go to school on foot*

**b.   Internal parts**

*Blood, teeth, tongue, saliva, heart, kidney, pancreas, Intestines, veins, grease, water, lungs and so on so forth*

*And so on so forth*

*ex:*

*1. Lungs help to breath*

*2.People speak thanks to their tongues*

*3.Generally teeth are red*

*4.The blood circulates in the veins*

*5.Oh no, sorry Maria Louisa, generally, teeth are white*

*6.Some people have red teeth*

*7.Uhu, it is u teeth fashion //Teeth are generally white*

*9. Generally, Teeth are red*

*10.Oh no generally teeth are white and the blood circulates in the veins*

*11.Ok you're right*

*12. Thank you*

*Song/Melody*

# Chapter Twenty Four / Two : Polite demands

1.Would you tell me your name Madam ?

2.Would you mind telling me your pre-name Sir?

3.Will you help me bring this luggage ?

4.Will you repeat after me ?

5.Can I have that green mango over there ?

6.May I go out Teacher ?

7.Shall we meet on the same time ?

8.Is it forbidden to smoke there ?

9.Are artists received in this room ?

10.May I sit on this chair ?

 Yes you may.

**Melody**

# **Chapter Twenty Five : Conjugation**

***a.Infinitive form:*** *to be, to have, to do, to go, to eat,*

*to play, to read, to travel, to love…*

***b.Simple present tense:***

*1. She plays basket -ball,*

*2. he reads a book // I like fresh fish // you need a black coffee*

*Remark: The verb takes s at the third person singular.*

 *ex: It rains, he corrects the test*

***c.Simple past tense:***

*1. She played basket -ball last day,*

*2.he passed his test yesterday*

*Remark: Regular verbs take ed to render the past tense.*

 *ex :*

*1.He continued reading Miller's book,*

 *2.We tried to convince her in vain,*

*3. Ahh,the doctor consulted the patient for two hours*

***d.Future tense:***

 *I will travel to London next week-end.*

 *Jane will be at home by night*

*Remark: In English the future tense is made with the modal will or shall.*

*ex:*

*1. Shall we go to Afraco for a film ? No we shan't.*

*2. It seems that they will defend their theses tomorrow morning.*

 *3.But I won't be there, I am going to have health check at the same hour.*

*4.Oh sorry.*

***e. Conditional form:***

*If I had money, I could travel to Antwerp.*

*If we were you, we could borrow money and trip to the States*

*Remark: If introduces the conditional form, consequently the verb works in the past.*

*ex:*

*1. If she had a free time, she would join us in the party.*

*2.If I had a car, I could see you off to the aeroplane*

**f. Present continuous tense**

*ex:*

*1. We are learning English,*

*2.Manda is going to church,*

*3. Melisa is swimming in the pool.*

*4. I am reading Shakespeare Romeo and Juliet.*

*5. You are attending a public lecture.*

*1. She is wearing a white hat,*

*2.He is canoeing to Bumba with his two kids*

*3. we are waiting for our wages.*

**Remark:** *The present continuous tense is made with the present tense of the verb to be plus any other verb in ing form.*

**g. past continuous tense:**

*1.I was coming to see you.*

*2.Ah yes you were driving a blue van.*

*3.That's it. But Brenda was playing piano in her room.*

*4. My parents were watching the football match in the living room.*

*Remark: The past continuous tense is made of the past of the verb to be plus any verb in ing form.*

*ex:*

*1.Arlene was singing Jackson 's song last evening,*

*2.They were attending a public lecture in the amphitheatre.*

***h. Present perfect tense:***

***ex:***

*1. I have finished my home –work .*

*2.You have completed yours an hour ago.*

*3.Indeed, Yvet has, always, been wise and prudent.*

*Remark: The present perfect tense is made of the present tense of the verb to have or to be plus any verb in the participial form*

***ex:***

*1 Minga has asked a difficult question to the teacher;*

*2 Marina has shouted during the exam.*

*3They have eaten evening meal early.*

*4.She is affected these days since she failed to the session*

*5.They were allowed to sit in the veranda*

***i.Past perfect tense:***

*1. I had received Dora's message,*

*2.She had sent it through WhatsApp.*

*3.They were taught German and Mandombe last year*

*4.He was kidnapped by gangsters*

***Remark:*** *The past perfect tense is made of the past tense of the verb to have or to be plus any verb in the participial form.*

***ex:***

*1.Mujinga had won the prize,*

*2.Twins had celebrated their birthday last week.*

*3.Roggers was received for a diner*

*4. Rooms were closed during the holiday*

***Song Melody***

# Chapter Twenty Six: Adverbs

*What are they ? They are modifiers or qualifiers*

*a. Adverbs of frequency:*

*Always, usually, sometimes, often, ever, never, etc.*

*ex: Christians, usually, go to church on Sunday*

*Sylvia and Enzo, often, meet in week-ends*

*No one has ever seen God.*

*Ehi they never see God*

*Remark: In general, frequency adverbs occur between the subject and the conjugated verb.*

*ex: God will, never, abandon sinners*

*Samba, usually, reads African playwrights*

### c.  Adverbs of manner

*They express or describe how things are done*

*ex: My father drives slowly. Slowly is an adverb of manner*

*This master teaches quickly. Ah this master teaches quickly. Oh yes, quickly is an adverb of manner*

*Remark: The adverb of manner modifies the verb in a sentence*

*ex: That athlete runs fast. Fast is, an adverb of manner, it modifies the verb to run.*

*The grand-parents speak wisely. Wisely is an adverb of manner, it qualifies the verb to speak.*

### c. Adverbs of quantity

*There are many ladies in this University. Please it's enough stop there;*

*No many, you know, is an adverb of quantity*

*Ok . When we say there are many ladies in this University, many in this sentence, stands for an adverb of quantity. Many is an adverb of quantity.*

*Please it's enough, stop there. Enough is an adverb of quantity too*

*Cardozo has much money. Much is an adverb of quantity.*

*Here are some adverbs of quantity: many, much, few, a few, enough, little, some, etc.*

**Song /Melody**

# Chapter Twenty-Seven: Sentence

*What is it?*

*It is a group of words organized containing a conjugated verb and revealing a meaningful statement.*

*There are three principal sorts of sentences: simple sentence, compound sentence and complex sentence*

*ex:*

*1. Come, go, I read a book, he is climbing up a tree,*

*2.Salima has been elected a national deputy*

*a.Simple sentence:*

*It contains one subject and one predicate*

*ex:*

*1.Trump rules USA*

*2.Trump is the subject. Rules USA is a predicate*

*3.The Pope Francis leads the universal Catholic church*

*4.The pope Francis is the subject*

*5.Leads the universal catholic church is a predicate*

***compound sentence:***

*It comprises two independent clauses linked by a conjunction of coordination.*

*ex:*

*1.Kabwamba plays football but Shakira plays volley ball*

*2.Mbenza hunts wild animals or he hunts savage birds*

*3.Mulimbi is my best student and his sister is my star in English*

***X. Some coordinating conjunctions:***

*but, or, and, either or, neither nor, …*

***c.Complex sentence:***

It is made of the main clause and one or more subordinate clauses thanks to a conjunction of subordination

ex:

1. As soon as the teacher gets in the class, the course starts

2.Mulumba goes back home because he feels sick

3.Sindano cannot travel to Europe until he gets his visa.

X. Here are some conjunctions of subordinations: till, until, unless, as soon as, because, for, yet, just, so, not only, but also, whether And so on so forth.

**Song /Melody**

# Chapter Twenty-Eight: Conjunctions+ Types

- *Conjunctions connect thoughts, actions, and ideas,*

- *They link nouns, clauses, and other parts of speech.*

*ex:*

*1. Mary went to the supermarket and bought oranges.*

- *Conjunctions are useful for making lists.*

 *ex:*

*1.Bwato's wife brought eggs, and coffee for breakfast.*

*2.Ah you want to say Bwato's wife brought eggs and coffee for breakfast?*

*3.Yeees*

*4.Okay, good*

**a.Types of Conjunctions**

*Many types of conjunctions with various roles within language structures.*

*Sorts of conjunctions: coordinating conjunctions, subordinating conjunctions, correlative conjunctions, Conjunctive adverbs*

*Here are some examples:*

**a.   Coordinating conjunction – or coordinators,**

*Coordinating conjunctions coordinate or join two or more sentences, main clauses, words, or other parts of speech which are of the same syntactic importance.*

*ex:You go out or you stay in*

 *Busaki teaches English but Bwama teaches chemistry*

**b.   Subordinating conjunctions or subordinators,**

*Subordinating conjunctions join dependent clauses to independent clauses.*

*ex: As soon as the priest gets in the church, the mass starts*

 *He wears a raincoat because it is raining*

### c.  *Correlative conjunctions*

These conjunctions correlate, while working in pairs, to join phrases or words that carry equal importance within a sentence.

ex: Either ... or, neither ... nor,

 ex: not only ... but also

ex.He is not only your coach but also your manager

They are all correlative conjunctions.

**Notes**: They recognize a correlative conjunction in that, when they see one, they, imperatively, see another. Not one without another.

ex.In the fall, Phillip will either start classes at the Building university college as his mother wishes or join the beach, his father's hope.

ex: Mianda cooked not only hot soja porridge but also burnt chicken meat for her darling Keko

**Melody/ Song**

# Chapter Twenty Nine: Prepositions

*A preposition is a word governing, and usually preceding, a noun or pronoun and expressing a relation to another word or element in the clause.*

*ex:*

*1." The man on the platform,"*

*2. "She arrived after dinner,"*

*3. "What did you do it for ?"*

**2.Sorts of prepositions:**

*There are three principal sorts of prepositions namely: prepositions of place, time and prepositions of direction.*

*a. Preposition of place: at, on, under, in, between, behind, near, next to, in front of, before, by, etc.*

*ex:*

*1.The teacher is in the classroom with students.*

*2. Pupils sit in front of their master*

*3.Sit by me, said Jesus*

*b. Prepositions of time: after, before, on, at etc.*

*ex:*

*1.The mouse dances after the cat has gone*

*2. Students must join the auditorium before the professor's arrival*

*3.The church service starts at six o'clock A M*

*c. Prepositions of directions: through, over, throughout, across, by, etc.*

*ex:*

*1.The thief entered throughout the window*

*2. The knife crossed through the apple*

*Notes: In English prepositions are used to connect nouns or between nouns and pronouns.*

*ex:*

*1. The maize behind the cock*

*2.The maize in front of the duck*

*3.The groundnut near the bird*

*4.The groundnut under the chicken*

*Notes: A preposition is used to show direction, location, or time, or to introduce an object.*

### 5. Prepositional phrases

***a.*** *Prepositional phrases consist of a preposition and the words which follow it (a complement).*

*The complement (underlined below) is most commonly a noun phrase or pronoun, but it can also be, an adverb phrase (usually one of place or time), a verb in the -ing form or, less commonly, a prepositional phrase or a wh-clause:*

*ex:*

*1.Toto and Lina first met at a party. (preposition + noun phrase)*

*2. Bimba was taken ill during the film. (preposition + noun phrase)*

*3. Would you like to come with me please? (preposition + pronoun)*

*4. From there, it'll take you about half an hour to our house. (preposition + adverb)*

*5.Until quite recently, no one knew about his paintings. (preposition + adverb phrase)*

*6.Samba has decided on doing a German language course. (preposition + -ing clause)*

*Not: Don't say, Samba decided on to do a German course/ that is Globish*

*7.It's a machine for making ice-cream. (preposition + -ing clause)*

*8.If you can wait until after my meeting with Jack, we can talk then. (preposition + prepositional phrase)*

*9.We were really surprised at what they wrote. (preposition + wh-clause)*

*Remark: An adverb can be put before a preposition to modify it. This applies mainly to prepositions of time or place which are gradable (above, before, far, deep, down, opposite etc.)*

*ex:*

*1.They've moved <u>far</u> into the country.*

*2.They left the party <u>just</u> before us.*

*3.You can't miss it.*

*4.Olenga's office is <u>almost</u> opposite the coffee machine.*

 ***Song// Melody***

**6.*Prepositional phrases after verbs***

*Prepositional phrases can be complements of verbs. Sometimes a special preposition is needed to introduce the complement of the verb. Such prepositional phrase is called 'prepositional verbs':*

*Do these keys belong to you?*

*We're not happy but we do approve of their decision.*

*We sometimes use an adverb particle before the preposition. The verb + adverb particle + preposition structure forms a verb which has a single meaning. We call such verbs 'phrasal prepositional verbs'. Their meaning is often not related to the meaning of the original verb:*

*Kukya really looks up to her grandfather. (admires)*

*Kids are all looking forward to having a few days' holiday together.*

# Chapter Thirty: A Prayer

*A prayer is an address (such as a petition) to God or a god in word or thought*

*One of the principal and common prayer is Our father.*

*Now let's pray Our Father:*

*Our Father:/ Our Father*

*Our Father who are in heaven ( he repeats)*

*Hallowed be your name*

*Your kingdom come*

*Your will be done on earth as it is in heaven*

*Give us this day our daily bread*

*And forgive us our trespasses*

*As we forgive those who trespass against us*

*Lead us not into temptations/ Don't leave us fall into temptation*

*But deliver us from evil*

*Amen*

***Song// Melody***

# Chapter Thirty-One: If you can't master English try Globish(2)

*What is Globish ?*

*It is a global English*

*How is it ?*
*Grammar is not important*
*Grammar is not important you say ?*

*Yes Globish does not take care of grammar*

*Oh yes, It takes less care to syntax*

*Euh sure ! what does it mean ?*

*It is not exactly English, but it works and does its job.*

*Message is sufficient, not grammar*

*Please avoid Globish, master English*

***Now you will be repeating after me***

*Repeat after me:* ***That is your homework***

*She sells sea shells by the sea shore(repeat)*

*Don't do that dad (repeat)*

*Stop teaching with teacher talk tough talks to talkative students (repeat)*

*Peter Pipper.................................................................................................*
*Good bye/*
*Bye bye.*
 ***Song //Melody***
 ***FOLLOW ME FOLLOW ME FOLLOW ME***

# References


BBC(1988),Getting on in English, British Broadcasting Corporation & Omnivox, Paris

Jon Hird/Paul Dummett with Harrison Sandy Millin,(2017)Keynote, Proficient, Workbook/National Geographical Learning, RR.Donnelley,

Liz S. & Soars JT F( 2003) Headway, Advanced workbook with key, OUP, London

- (2009)New Headway, Advanced Student's Book, OUP, London

Schoenberg I E (1994),Focus on Grammar, A Basic course for Reference and Practice,Addison-WesleyPublishing Company,Massachussets, Newyork

Suzan N.( 1999 ),We mean business, An elementary course in business English, Students' Book, Longman, London

Swan M,& Walter C.(1986),The Cambridge English Course, Students' Book, CUP, London

Take Over 1,( 2011) English, ELV-Hoorelbeke Christelle Foissac Patrick, Namur

Van der Walt & al (2011) Basic Skills in Academic Literacy, 3$^{rd}$ edition, Potchefstroom

Vermeulen, J( 2012),Email for College and Business, Academia Press, Gent

Werner-U.D.(2004) Assimil, l'Anglais Britannique de Poche. Chennevières –sur-Marnes Cedex, Paris